Standards-Based Connections
Reading
Grade K

Carson-Dellosa Publishing, LLC
Greensboro, North Carolina

Credits

Content Editor: Jeanette M. Ritch, MS Ed
Copy Editor: Christine M. Schwab

Visit *carsondellosa.com* for correlations to Common Core, state, national, and Canadian provincial standards.

Carson-Dellosa Publishing, LLC
PO Box 35665
Greensboro, NC 27425 USA
carsondellosa.com

ISBN 978-1-4838-2473-4

01-188151151

Table of Contents

Introduction

Reading comprehension is an essential skill for enabling school, college, and career success. This book focuses on five reading comprehension skills: story elements, summarizing, compare and contrast, cause and effect, and inferring. Emphasized are the reading standards in the Common Core State Standards.

The reading standards set expectations for each grade level and define what students should understand and be able to do. They are designed to be more rigorous and allow for students to justify their thinking. They reflect the knowledge that is necessary for success in college and career readiness. Students who master the standards as they advance through the grades exhibit the following capabilities:

1. They demonstrate independence.
2. They build strong content knowledge.
3. They respond to the varying demands of audience, task, purpose, and discipline.
4. They comprehend as well as critique.
5. They value evidence.
6. They use technology and digital media strategically and capably.
7. They come to understand other perspectives and cultures.*

How to Use This Book

This book is a collection of grade-appropriate practice pages aligned to the reading sections of the Common Core State Standards for English Language Arts. Included is a skill matrix to show exactly which standards are addressed on the practice pages. Also included are a skill assessment and a skill assessment analysis. Use the assessment at the beginning of the year or at any time you wish to assess your students' mastery of certain standards. The analysis connects each test item to a practice page or set of practice pages so that you can review skills with students who struggle in certain areas.

Common Core State Standards Alignment Matrix

Page #	12	13	14	15	16	17	18	19	20	21	22	23	24	25	26	27	28	29	30	31	32	33	34	35	36	37	38	39	40	41	42	43	44	45	46	47	48	49	50	51
K.RL.1			•	•							•	•		•	•		•	•	•						•					•		•	•							
K.RL.2																			•											•										
K.RL.3			•		•			•		•		•	•			•																								
K.RL.4				•																																				
K.RL.5									•						•										•															
K.RL.6																																								
K.RL.7	•	•	•		•	•	•		•				•		•	•	•	•										•												
K.RL.8																																								
K.RL.9																																								
K.RL.10						•	•	•																	•		•													
K.RI.1																				•	•	•	•	•	•		•	•					•					•		•
K.RI.2																						•	•	•		•														
K.RI.3																																	•	•	•	•		•	•	•
K.RI.4																					•																			
K.RI.5																																								
K.RI.6																																								
K.RI.7																				•													•			•	•		•	•
K.RI.8																							•																	
K.RI.9																										•									•					
K.RI.10																					•																	•		

Page #	52	53	54	55	56	57	58	59	60	61	62	63	64	65	66	67	68	69	70	71	72	73	74	75	76	77	78	79	80	81	82	83	84	85	86	87	88	89	90	91
K.RL.1		•								•				•	•	•	•	•	•	•	•	•	•	•		•	•	•					•					•		
K.RL.2										•																•	•	•												
K.RL.3							•	•			•	•	•	•						•	•	•				•	•	•	•	•	•			•		•	•	•		
K.RL.4																																								
K.RL.5						•			•																															
K.RL.6							•																																	
K.RL.7		•				•	•	•			•	•											•							•	•	•	•	•	•		•		•	•
K.RL.8																																								
K.RL.9						•	•	•															•	•					•											
K.RL.10																																								
K.RI.1											•								•								•													
K.RI.2			•																																					
K.RI.3			•		•						•																													
K.RI.4																																								
K.RI.5																																								
K.RI.6			•																																					
K.RI.7				•															•																•					
K.RI.8																																								
K.RI.9	•			•																																				
K.RI.10	•																																							

The Loris and the Raccoon

Have you ever seen a loris? It is an animal. It is small. It looks like a raccoon. It is soft. It has big eyes. It eats at night. It is cute. But, it has poison. The poison is in its bite. Poison is a liquid that can hurt. Yikes!

The raccoon is an animal. It does not have poison. It likes the night. It is also soft. It does not have big eyes. Some people think raccoons are cute.

1. How are the animals alike? _____

2. How are the animals different? _____

3. Which animal has poison in its bite? _____

4. Look at the raccoon. Where are its stripes? _____

5. What are the main topics of this passage? _____

6. What is a liquid that can hurt? _____

Dom and Kay

Dom and Kay are good friends. They have different hair. They have different eyes. But, they are so much alike. They like to play outside. They run in the yard. They like to ride their bikes. They go to school too. They are in the same class. Dom wrote a poem for Kay. It said:

When we play,
We have so much fun.
You are my friend.
You are my number one!

7. How are the girls alike? _____

8. How are the girls different? _____

9.   What did Dom write for Kay? _____

10.   Who is the author, or the writer, of the poem? _____

11.   Where do they play? _____

12.   Tell what they do outside. _____

13.   Find a friend. Talk about what it means to be a good friend.
      Write a sentence. _____

      _____

At the Beach
By Jeanette M. Ritch

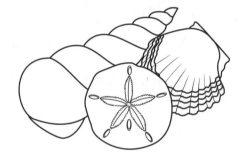

Did you ever go to a beach? A beach can be next to the sea. Shells are at the beach. A shell is on a sea animal. One sea animal is called a mollusk. A mollusk is safe because of the shell. It is like a skeleton. A sea snail has a shell. Shells are fun to find. They are pretty too. They can have lots of colors.

14.   What are some sea animals called? _____

15.   Write a new title for the story. _____

16.   An artist made the picture of some shells. Who wrote the passage?

      _____

17.   Why does the author think shells are pretty? _____

18.   Find a friend. Talk about the beach. Write a sentence.

      _____

      _____

Picture Perfect

19.   Mark is on a trip. Read Mark's postcard to his friend Jeff. Draw a picture in the box of the place where Mark is.

Dear Jeff,

   We are here! I swam in this blue lake. My dad and I hiked to that mountain! My mom took a picture in front of this big tall tree. This place is fun!

                Your friend,
                Mark

Jeff Hilton

5555 Brighten Road

Portville, Oregon 97321

Happy or Sad?

20. How does the person feel? Draw a happy face or sad face in each box.

Kitten

Sally is a baby cat. A baby cat is called a kitten. Sally has yellow fur. She lives in a house. She lives with a family. The family feeds Sally. They play with her too. Sally loves to live with the family!

21. Who is Sally? _____

22. Where does she live? _____

23. What does she love? _____

24. What is a kitten? _____

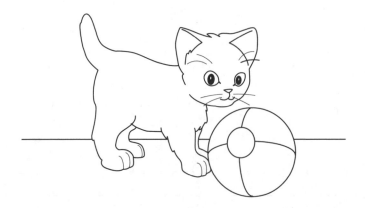

Liv at the Doctor

Liv went to the doctor. Her hand hurt. She was scared. She had to get her hand checked. The doctor was nice. She talked to Liv's mom and dad. She said Liv needed surgery. Surgery is when a doctor fixes the body. The doctor fixed Liv's hand. Liv was a brave girl. She felt better!

25. What is surgery? _____

26. Whom did the doctor talk to? _____

27. How did Liv feel at first? _____

28. How did she feel at the end of the story? _____

29. Look at the picture. Do you think the doctor looks kind? _____

Big Waves

Read the story. Read each pair of sentences. Circle the word **Cause** by the sentence that tells about the cause. Circle the word **Effect** by the sentence that tells about the effect.

Have you ever thrown a rock in a pond? Did you see waves circle out from the place where the rock hit the water?

When there is an earthquake in the ocean, big waves go out from the place where it happened. There are several waves, not just one.

Fishermen on two boats saw very big waves near Alaska. They went over the waves in their boats. They were safe!

30. Waves go out from the place where the rock fell in the water.   Cause   Effect

You throw a rock into a pond.   Cause   Effect

31. Fishermen went over the waves. They were safe.   Cause   Effect

The fishermen were in their boats when the big waves came.   Cause   Effect

Where Am I?

Read the sentences below. Use clues in the sentences to infer where each person is.

32. Stacie rode the merry-go-round. She flew high on the swings. She rode down the slide.
     Where is Stacie? _____

33. Tina walked in the door. She sat down at her desk. He got out her book. She read. Her teacher told her to put the book away. It was time for art.

     Where is Tina? _____

Shopping

Yin was hungry! Dad did not go shopping. The fridge was empty. So, Dad went to shop. He put fruit in his cart. He paid for it all. He came home. Yin ate the fresh fruit. Now, Yin is full!

34. Why did Dad go to shop? _____

35. How did Yin feel at the end of the story? _____

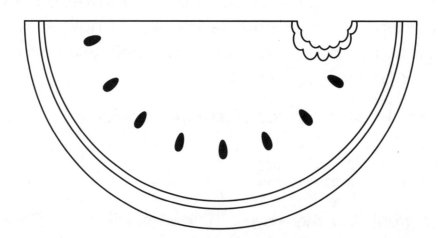

After you review the results of your student's skill assessment, match those problems answered incorrectly to the reading comprehension skills below. Pay special attention to the pages that fall into these problem sections and ensure that your student receives supervision in these areas. In this way, your student will strengthen these skills.

Answer Key: 1. They look alike, are soft, are awake at night. 2. The loris has poison and big eyes. The raccoon does not. 3. loris; 4. tail; 5. loris, raccoon; 6. poison. 7. play outside, ride bikes, same class; 8. different hair, eyes; 9. a poem; 10. Dom; 11. outside; 12. ride bikes, run in the yard; 13. Answers will vary. 14. mollusks; 15. Answers will vary. 16. Jeanette M. Ritch; 17. colors; 18–19. Answers will vary. 20. sad, happy; 21. kitten; 22. house; 23. to live with a family; 24. baby cat; 25. when the doctor fixes the body; 26. Liv's mom and dad; 27. scared; 28. better; 29. yes; 30. Effect, Cause; 31. Effect, Cause; 32. playground; 33. school; 34. The fridge was empty. 35. He felt full.

Comprehension Skill	Common Core State Standards*	Assessment Item(s)	Practice Page(s)
Reading Standards for Literature			
Story Elements	K.RL.1, K.RL.3, K.RL.5, K.RL.7, K.RL.10	19, 21–24, 26–28	12–30, 36, 42, 48, 51, 52, 57, 60, 72–75, 77–79, 82, 85, 87, 89
Summarizing	K.RL.1, K.RL.2, K.RL.7	9–13	14, 15, 21–23, 25, 28–30, 36, 39, 41–43, 58–61, 78–80, 84
Compare and Contrast	K.RL.6, K.RL.7, K.RL.10	7, 8	16–19, 24, 53, 57–59, 76, 77, 79, 91
Cause and Effect	K.RL.1, K.RL.3, K.RL.7	34–35	60, 61, 63–69, 72–75
Inferring	K.RL.1, K.RL.3, K.RL.4, K.RL.7	20, 25, 29, 32, 33	15, 33, 76–85, 87–91
Reading Standards for Informational Text			
Story Elements	K.RI.1, K.RI.5, K.RI.7, K.RI.10	16	31, 33–35, 38–40, 44, 45, 48, 49, 51, 52, 56, 70, 71
Summarizing	K.RI.1, K.RI.2, K.RI.3, K.RI.6, K.RI.8	5, 15	31–35, 37, 38, 40, 47, 54, 55
Compare and Contrast	K.RI.3, K.RI.5, K.RI.6, K.RI.9	1–4, 18	37, 40, 44–52, 54–56
Cause and Effect	K.RI.1, K.RI.3, K.RI.8	30, 31	35, 62, 70, 71
Inferring	K.RI.1, K.RI.4	6, 14, 17	33, 86

* © Copyright 2010 National Governors Association Center for Best Practices and Council of Chief State School Officers. All rights reserved.

Story Titles

Each picture has a character. The title of the first picture is "Sue Goes to the Store." Write a title for each picture.

1. Sue Goes to the Store

2. _____

   _____

3. _____

   _____

4. _____

   _____

☐   **I can tell how the story and the pictures go together.**

Who Am I?

Read each story. Cut out the pictures. Glue the picture by the correct story.

1. He hopped out of the oven.

   He ran and ran so fast.

   No one could catch him.

2. He climbed up and up the waterspout.

   The rain washed him out.

   He climbed again.

3. She wanted to bake bread.

   She asked the animals to help.

   No one helped her.

   But, they all wanted to eat her bread!

4. He went out with his mother and father.

   They found a little girl in their home.

   The girl was sleeping in his bed.

☐   I can tell how the story and the pictures go together.

CD-104657

13

Story Time

Every story has characters.

A story character can be a or who runs and plays.

Or, a story character can be a or a .

Maybe the character is a or a .

Sometimes, characters are happy. Sometimes, they are sad.
Reading about them can be fun!

Look at pictures from three stories you know. Write the correct answer on the line.

1. _____

   Whom is this story about?

   three birds and a boy   three bears and a girl

2. _____

   Whom is this story about?

   a woman   a man

3. _____

   Whom are the characters in this story?

   a girl and a wolf   a boy and a cat

☐ I can ask and answer questions about what I read.
☐ I can name the characters, settings, and events in a story.
☐ I can tell how the story and the pictures go together.

Baby Fox

Read the story. Answer the questions.

Tommy is a baby fox. A baby fox is called a kit. Tommy has red fur. He lives with his mother in the woods. Their home is called a **den**. Tommy and his mother hunt for food to eat. Tommy loves the woods!

1. Who is Tommy?

   _____

   _____

2. What is a den?

   _____

   _____

3. What does Tommy love?

   _____

   _____

☐ I can ask and answer questions about what I read.
☐ I can ask and answer questions about words I do not know in a story.

Where Do Stories Take Place?

Read the story about settings. Use the picture to answer each question.

The place a story happens is the **setting.** A setting can be a real place like a  or a . Sometimes, the setting is make-believe. A princess may live in a castle. A bird may live in a nest. A story about a bat may take place in a cave. A story about a boy may take place in a park.

1. Draw a circle around the setting for a .

2. Draw a square around the setting for a .

3. Draw an X on the setting for a .

4. Draw a line under the setting for a  .

☐ I can name the characters, settings, and events in a story.
☐ I can tell how the story and the pictures go together.

In the Picture

Draw a setting in each box.

1.

2.

3.

4.

Group Activity: Find friends in your class. Show your settings. Talk about them.

☐ I can tell how the story and the pictures go together.
☐ I can take part in group reading activities.

Out of Place

Look at each setting. Cross out the picture that does not belong.

Group Activity: Find a friend in your class. Make a story about one set of pictures. Talk about it or write it.

☐ I can tell how the story and the pictures go together.
☐ I can take part in group reading activities.

How Do You Feel?

A story has characters and settings that can make you feel happy or sad.
Draw a line from each picture to the word that tells how it makes you feel.

happy

sad

Group Activity: Find a friend. Talk about a setting that makes you feel happy. Draw a picture of it.

❑   I can tell how the story and the pictures go together.
❑   I can take part in group reading activities.

Do You Know the Time?

The setting tells us when the story takes place. Look at each month. The months are part of a calendar. Read each clue. Write each letter in the correct month. The pictures can help you make matches.

A.   in art class making hearts

B.   in a field building a snowman

C.   in a yard raking the leaves

D.   in a park with butterflies

E.   on a beach eating fruit

F.   in a kitchen baking a turkey

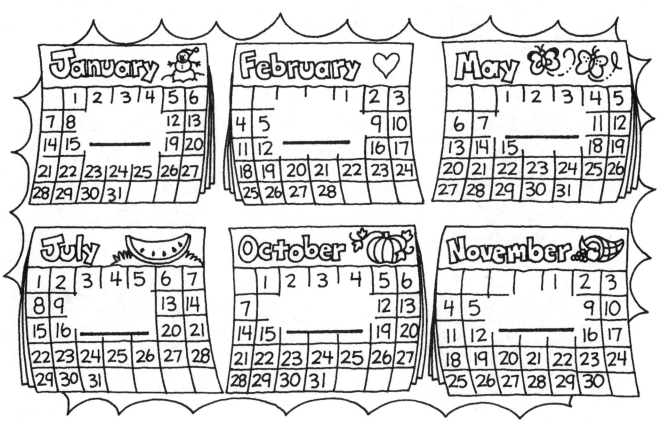

☐   I can name the characters, settings, and events in a story.
☐   I can tell the difference between stories, poems, and other things to read.

Get the Picture

Look at each setting. Choose the correct words from the word bank. Write them on the lines.

Word Bank

ball	bats	clouds	ice
rocket	stars	trees	water

1.

_____

2.

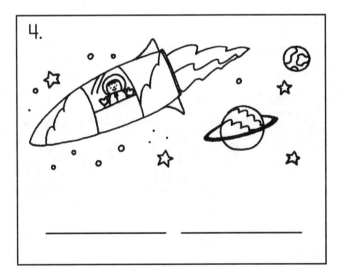

_____

3.

_____ _____

4.

_____ _____

☐ I can tell how the story and the pictures go together.

Time Travel

The setting tells us when a story takes place. Read each story sentence. When did each story take place? Draw an **X** in the correct box.

	Long Ago	Today	Future
1. Tracy put on her helmet. She rode her bike along the trail.			
2. Yuri looked at the stars around him. He lived in a green pod. He rode a rocket bus to school.			
3. It was Laura's first train ride. She watched the other wagons come to the station. The train left the station.			
4. Zach's family parked their mini-van in the big lot. They crossed a red bridge to the park.			

❑   I can ask and answer questions about what was read.
❑   I can name the characters, settings, and events in a story.

Where Are We?

Read each story. Choose the correct setting from the word bank. Write it on the line.

Word Bank

forest   outer space

1. Chet was hungry. He ran down the tree trunk. He dug in the leaves. He wanted the nut he hid yesterday. He dug and dug. It was not there! He looked at the other trees. Where did he hide the nut?

_____

2. Miguel looked out the window. He saw Earth behind him. It looked very small. Then, he looked at Pluto. That is where he is going. He will like his new home.

_____

☐ **I can ask and answer questions about what was read.**

Who Said That?

Read each sentence. Write the correct character's name on the line.

1. "Hey! I am angry," said _____.

2. "I am bored," said _____.

3. "That loud noise scared me," said _____.

4. "Mom and I are going to the beach," said _____.

5. "I can't find my favorite toy," said _____.

Time for Dan

Read the story. Circle the word that tells about each character.

Dan wanted something. He ran to find Tyler. Tyler was reading a book. Dan walked up the stairs to Holly's bedroom. She was playing a game. She did not look to see what Dan wanted.

Dan ran back down the steps. He got his leash. He went to Tyler. This time, Tyler put his book down. "What do you want, boy?" Tyler asked.

Dan ran to the door. He wagged his tail. Tyler put on his coat. He said, "Holly, do you want to go outside with us?"

"Yes," said Holly.

1. Dan

    boy   girl   dog

2. Tyler

    boy   girl   dog

3. Holly

    boy   girl   dog

❑ I can ask and answer questions about what was read.
❑ I can name the characters, settings, and events in a story.

Name_____

The Hunters

Read the rebus. Circle a picture to answer each question.

 asked her for some . She packed the , some  , and in her 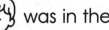 . She was going on

a hunting trip. walked to the . was in the

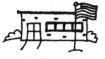 too. He had a . and wanted to find

something to show at  . saw an . She drew

the with her and . saw a . He took

a picture of the with his  . shared her with .

1. Who took the 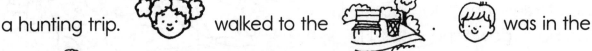 to the  ?

2. Who had a ?

3. Who took a backpack to the  ?

4. Who saw an ?

5. Who saw a  ?

☐ I can ask and answer questions about what was read.
☐ I can tell the difference between stories, poems, and other things to read.
☐ I can tell how the story and the pictures go together.

Here Is My Story

Look at the pictures. Circle the character's name. Underline the best title for each story.

1. Myong

   Kami

   Ruff

Kami Washes Dishes   Kami Makes a Mask

2. Myong

   Kami

   Ruff

Myong Flies a Kite   Myong Does Homework

3. Myong

   Kami

   Ruff

Ruff Plays Catch   Ruff Finds a Bone

☐   I can name the characters, settings, and events in a story.
☐   I can tell how the story and the pictures go together.

Name_____

Lucy and Rosa

Read the story. Circle the correct word to answer each question. Color the pictures of the two friends.

Friends are special. Lucy and Rosa are friends. They ride the bus to school. They go to the fair. They help each other read. They are happy to be friends.

1. What is the story about?

    fair   friends   books

2. What word describes friends?

    bus   read   special

☐   I can ask and answer questions about what was read.
☐   I can tell how the story and the pictures go together.

28

© Carson-Dellosa • CD-104657

Time for School

Read the story. Circle the correct picture to answer each question.

Andy is happy! He has a new backpack. It is red and blue.
He puts pencils, crayons, a ruler, and a pencil box in his new backpack. Andy is ready for school.

1. Who is excited?

2. What does Andy have in his backpack?

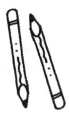    

3. What is Andy getting ready for?

☐ I can ask and answer questions about what was read.

Growing

Read the story. Look at the pictures. Circle the correct answer for each question.

Josie had a rattle when she was a baby. She loved to shake it! It made noise. Josie had a bear when she was three. It was her favorite toy. Now, Josie is five years old. Tomorrow is her first day of school. She is a big girl!

1. What is the best title for this story?

    Baby Josie   Josie Grows Up   Funny Pictures

2. What happened to Josie in the story?

    She grew older.

    She looked at pictures.

    She went home.

Retell the story. Fill in the blanks.

3. Josie is now _____.

4. Tomorrow, she will go to _____.

☐ I can ask and answer questions about what was read.
☐ I can retell a story.

Home, Sweet Home

Read the passage. Circle the correct word to complete each sentence.
Write the word on the line.

Every animal has a home. Animals make their homes in different places. Birds make nests in trees or on the ground. Bees make hives in trees or under the ground. Ants and moles make homes under the ground. Bears and bats are in caves.

1. Every animal has a _____.

    pillow   car   home

2. Some animals build homes in _____.

    trees   trucks   boxes

3. Some animals have homes under the _____.

    apples   ground   street

4. Other animals have homes in _____.

    caves   cones   wheels

☐ I can ask and answer questions about what I read.

Making Sense of It

Read the story. Answer each question.

Clink, clink, clink! Your ears hear.

Your eyes see.

Your nose smells.

Your hands feel.

Your tongue tastes.

Your five senses help you enjoy your world!

1. What would be a good title for this story?

   A Picnic　　　　　　　Hot Dogs　　　　　　　Helpful Senses

2. How many senses do you have?

   three　　　　　　　　five　　　　　　　　six

3. Which part of your body helps you hear?

4. Which part of your body helps you smell?

☐　I can ask and answer questions about what I read.
☐　I can tell how the pictures and the words go together.

What Is a Month?

Read the passage. Answer each question.

There are 12 months in a year. The word month is from the word moon. The moon goes around Earth about once each month. Most months have 30 or 31 days. February is different. That month usually has 28 days. Every four years, February has 29 days. That is called a **leap year**.

1. Write a new title for this story.

   _____

2. What is one thing you learned?

   _____

   _____

   _____

3. What is a **leap year**?

   _____

   _____

☐ I can ask and answer questions about what I read.
☐ I can tell the topic and details of a story.
☐ I can ask and answer questions about words I do not know in a story.

Big Hairy Spiders

Read the passage. Answer each question.

A tarantula is a big spider. It is hairy. It is scary. Many people are afraid. But, spiders are afraid of us too! They like to hide under rocks. They hide in tunnels.

If you scare tarantulas, they give a kick. Why? They have tiny hairs on their bellies. They can kick the hairs from their bellies. The hairs act like little arrows.

1. What does the passage say is the same about people and tarantulas?

    _____

2. Where do tarantulas hide?

    _____

3. What is this article about?

    _____

    _____

    _____

Group Activity: Turn to a friend. Ask if your friend has ever seen a spider.

☐ I can ask and answer questions about what I read.
☐ I can tell the topic and details of a story.
☐ I can take part in group reading activities.

Who Was Johnny Appleseed?

Read the passage. Answer each question.

John Chapman lived long ago. He loved apples. He moved to the West. He brought apple seeds. Not many people lived there. Only a few farmers grew apples.

John wanted to grow apple trees. He cut down bushes. He planted his seeds. His trees started to grow. More people came to the West. They wanted to grow apples. John sold his trees. People called him Johnny Appleseed.

1. Who is this story about?

    _____

    _____

    _____

2. Why is John Chapman called Johnny Appleseed?

    _____

    _____

    _____

3. Why did the author write that only a few farmers grew apples?

    _____

    _____

    _____

☐ I can ask and answer questions about what I read.
☐ I can tell the topic and details of a story.
☐ I can tell what the author is thinking and why.

Where Is Sassy?

Read with a friend. Answer each question. Draw a picture of Sassy in the box.

Sassy is missing!

Sassy is a cat with orange, black, and white spots. She has yellow eyes. She has a blue collar with a tag. Please call Kit at 555-2134 if you see Sassy. Thank you!

1. What is this?

   a newspaper ad

   a poster

   a book

2. Who has lost something?

   a store

   a dog

   a girl

❑ **I can ask and answer questions about what was read.**
❑ **I can tell the difference between stories, poems, and other things to read.**
❑ **I can take part in group reading activities.**

What Is a Day?

Read each passage. Make an **X** by the best title for each.

1. There are 24 hours in a day. That is how long it takes Earth to turn once. It is day when our part of Earth faces the sun. It is night when our part of Earth turns away from the sun.

    ○ What Makes Day and Night

    ○ All About the Sun

2. In the summer, days are long and nights are short. In the winter, days are short and nights are long. Seasons change because of the way Earth moves. Our part of Earth is closer to the sun in the summer. Our part of Earth is farther from the sun in the winter.

    ○ Summer Fun

    ○ Earth and the Seasons

3. How are these two passages the same?

    _____

☐ I can ask and answer questions about what I read.
☐ I can compare two stories.

Name_____

What Is a Week?

Read the passage. Answer each question.

There are seven days in a week. The first day is Sunday. It is named after the sun. The second day of the week is Monday. Can you guess what it is named after? You are right! Monday is named after the moon.

Tuesday, Wednesday, and Thursday come in the middle of the week. Friday is at the end. Saturday is on the weekend. On Sunday, it is a brand new week. We start all over again!

1. Write a new title for this passage.

   _____

2. What is one thing you learned?

   _____

   _____

   _____

❑ I can ask and answer questions about what I read.
❑ I can tell the topic and the details of a story.

Name_____

How Many Bugs?

Read the story. Complete the activity on page 40.

Maya and Carl are friends. One afternoon, they went to see what they could find in Carl's garden.

"We can find bugs," Maya said. "Count everything that we find!"

They did find bugs. Carl found 4 ants, 3 butterflies, 2 bees, 7 ladybugs, 4 flies, and a grasshopper. Maya found 5 ants, 2 butterflies, a bee, 3 ladybugs, a grasshopper—and no at all.

"I win," Carl cried out, adding up bugs in his head. "I found 21 bugs in all."

"Good job," said Maya.

☐ I can take part in reading activities.

How Many Bugs? (cont.)

Cut out the bug pictures. Glue the correct picture in each box. Answer the questions.

1. Maya saw more  than anything else.

2. Carl saw more 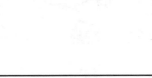 than anything else.

3. They both saw the same number of  .

4. What do Maya and Carl like to do?

_____

5. What did they look for in the garden?

_____

❑ I can ask and answer questions about what I read.
❑ I can retell a story.

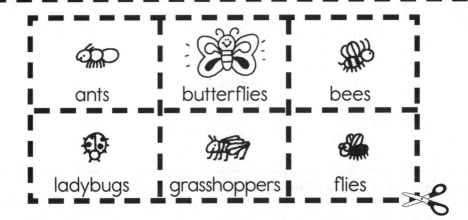

Fun at the Park

Look at each picture. Read the word. Use three of the words to complete the sentence.

swings   slide   car

bars   ice skates   merry-go-round

I went to the park. I played on the _____,

_____, and _____.

I had a lot of fun!

☐ **I can tell how the story and pictures go together.**

Party Time!

Read the story. Color the correct picture to answer each question. Write a word from the story to complete the sentence.

Ann is having a party.

Her friends are at her house.

There are balloons at the party.

There is pizza for everyone.

All of Ann's friends have a good time!

1. Who is the story about?

2. What do people eat at the party?

3. Ann is having a _____ party.

Pet Shopping

Look at each picture. Read the word. Use three of the words to complete the sentence.

kite	collar	book
bed	fish bowl	dog dish

Dusty is our dog. We want to get him a new_____,

_____, and _____.

He needs them.

Bug Off!

Read about bugs. Read the words in the middle of the page. Circle the traits that belong to both insects and people. Draw lines to match the words to the bug or the person.

Some bugs are insects! They have **skeletons** like you do. But, an insect's skeleton is outside its body. Yours is inside. Bugs have three body parts. A bug has a **head**, just like you do. People do not have **wings**. Some insects have **wings** so that they can fly. Insects have **legs**, but they do not look like your **legs**! They have **six** legs instead of two. They also have **two kinds of eyes**!

A.

1. skeleton inside

2. skeleton outside

3. head

4. legs

5. six legs

6. two legs

7. two eyes

8. two kinds of eyes

9. wings

B.

☐   I can tell how two people, places, or things are connected in a story.
☐   I can tell how the pictures and the words go together.

Dogs and Cats

Read each sentence. Circle **same** or **different**.

1. Dogs and cats are animals.   same   different

2. Dogs bark, and cats meow.   same   different

3. Dogs and cats have four feet.   same   different

4. Baby cats are called kittens,
   while baby dogs are called puppies.   same   different

5. Cats can climb in trees, but most dogs cannot.   same   different

6. Dogs and cats can be good pets.   same   different

7. Most dogs and cats have fur.   same   different

8. Cats purr, and dogs do not.   same   different

❑   I can ask and answer questions about what I read.
❑   I can tell how two people, places, or things are connected in a story.

Shape Up

Look at each row. Color the leaves that are alike in each row.

© Carson-Dellosa • CD-104657

What Is New?

Look at each picture. What has been added to the nest? Write the correct words from the word bank.

Word Bank

| baby birds | eggs | leaves |

1.

2.

3.

☐ I can tell how two people, places, or things are connected in a story.
☐ I can tell how the pictures and the words go together.

Match Them Up!

Circle the shape that is different in each row.

A.

B.

C.

Group Activity: Shapes are in every room. They are outside too. Shapes are everywhere! Find a friend. Look around. Write three shapes you see.

_____

_____

_____

☐   I can tell how the pictures and the words go together.
☐   I can take part in group reading activities.

Name_____

Flag Day

Color each flag. Circle the correct answer to each question.

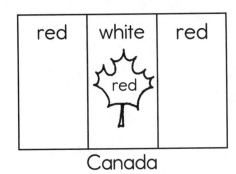

red	white	red
	red	

Canada

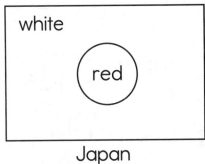

white

red

Japan

red
white
dark blue

The Netherlands

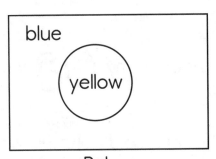

blue

yellow

Palau

1. Look at the two red and white flags. What shape is on Japan's flag?

2. What shape is on Canada's flag?

3. Look at the two flags with blue parts. Palau's flag has a _____ ◯.

    white   red   yellow

☐ I can ask and answer questions about what I read.
☐ I can tell how two people, places, or things are connected in a story.

Too Hot! Too Cold!

Circle **too hot** or **too cold** to complete each sentence.

1. I put on a if I feel   too hot   too cold.

2. I turn on a when it is   too hot   too cold.

3. I swim in the when it is   too hot   too cold.

4. I put on my  when I am   too hot   too cold.

5. I drink cold when I am   too hot   too cold.

☐   **I can tell how two people, places, or things are connected in a story.**
☐   **I can tell how the pictures and the words go together.**

Name_____

What Is the Weather?

Look at each picture. Answer the questions.

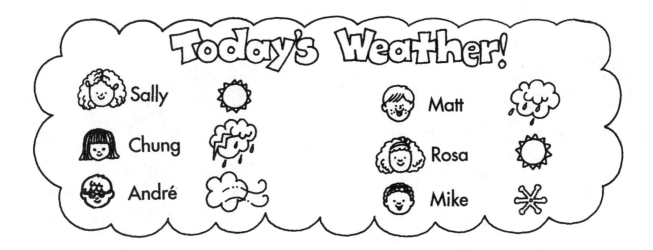

1. Who will have sunny weather? _____

2. Who will have rain? _____

3. Who will have windy weather? _____

4. Who will need an umbrella today?_____

   _____

5. Who should wear mittens and a hat today? _____

❑ I can ask and answer questions about what I read.
❑ I can tell how two people, places, or things are connected in a story.
❑ I can tell how the pictures and the words go together.

What Is Different?

Sit with a friend. Say the four words in each pumpkin. One word does not sound the same as the other three. Cross out the one that is different.

1. look
   book
   boat
   took

2. bat
   man
   hat
   that

3. bill
   will
   tin
   pill

4. got
   sun
   run
   fun

5. all
   jam
   tall
   ball

6. ten
   men
   sat
   then

7. dog
   toy
   boy
   joy

8. mop
   dig
   pig
   big

❑ I can compare words that are alike and different.
❑ I can take part in group reading activities.

Short, Tall, Big, Small

Put the kids in order from tallest to shortest. Write **1** for the tallest. Write **5** for the shortest. Circle the correct word in each sentence.

Lei _____ Anna _____ Javon _____ Bill _____ José _____

1. Lei is   taller   shorter   than Javon.

2. Anna is the   tallest   shortest.

3. Javon is   taller   shorter   than Bill.

4. Bill is the   tallest   shortest.

❑ I can ask and answer questions about what I read.
❑ I can tell how the pictures and the words go together.

Big Sharks and Whales

Read the passage. Use the facts to complete the chart on the next page. Answer the question below.

A giant whale shark is big! It cannot fit on a bus. The biggest tiger shark is as long as a car. A hammerhead shark is shorter than a tiger shark but weighs the same.

A great blue whale can weigh almost as much as a train. A blue whale can be longer than two buses!

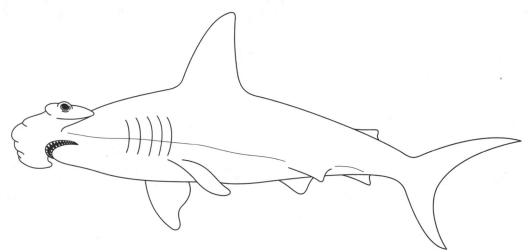

The author is the writer.

The author writes the facts.

The illustrator is the artist.

The illustrator makes the art.

1. Why do the author and illustrator need each other? _____

_____

_____

❑ I can tell how two people, places, or things are connected in a story.
❑ I can name the author and illustrator and tell what they do.

Big Sharks and Whales (cont.)

Complete the chart.

Fact

1. whale shark	
2. tiger shark	
3. hammerhead shark	
4. blue whale	

5.   Write a sentence about a shark. _____

_____

_____

6.   Write a sentence about a whale. _____

_____

_____

❑ **I can tell the topic and details of a story.**
❑ **I can compare two stories.**

Two Legs, Four Legs, or Six Legs?

Cut out the pictures. Glue each picture in the correct column.

2 Legs	4 Legs	6 Legs

☐ I can name the characters in a story.
☐ I can tell how the pictures and the words go together.

City or Country

Read each sentence. Cut out the sentence strips. Glue each sentence in the correct box to make two stories.

City	Country

- ❑ I can tell the difference between stories, poems, and other things to read.
- ❑ I can tell how the story and the pictures go together.
- ❑ I can compare characters and events from different stories.

1. The  looks at the .   4. The brings home the .

2. The drives a .   5. The walks into the .

3. The sees a .   6. A rides in a .

Animal Riddles

Read each riddle. Choose the correct animal name. Write it on the line.

Word Bank

bear   giraffe   seal

1. I am big and furry, and I live in a cave. I like to sleep all winter long. I also like to eat honey!	2. I have shiny black fur. I love to swim and dive in the water. I eat fish. I can even do tricks.	3. I have four legs and a very long neck. My long neck helps me eat leaves from tall trees. I have big brown spots.
I am a _____.	I am a _____.	I am a _____.

Read the passage. Answer the question.

The author is the writer. The author writes the riddles.
The illustrator is the artist. The illustrator makes the art.

4. Why do they need each other? _____

_____

❑ I can tell about the author and the illustrator of the story.
❑ I can tell how the story and the pictures go together.
❑ I can compare characters and events from different stories.

More Animal Riddles

Riddles give clues. Read each clue. Cut out the animal pictures. Glue the correct picture in each box.

1. I can live in the water or on land.	2. I do not have legs, and I cannot fly.	3. I have a mane.
4. I have spots, and I give milk.	5. I have whiskers, and I drink milk.	6. I have two legs, and I can fly.

☐ I can tell how the story and the pictures go together.
☐ I can compare characters and events from different stories.

A. cow   B. bird   C. frog

D. snake   E. lion   F. cat

In the News

News titles tell the effect. News stories tell the cause. Read the titles. Choose the best title for each story. Write it on the line.

> **Titles**
> Boy Saves Dog
> Grass Turns Brown
> Kids Clean Up

1. The kids made a mess at the school picnic. Their teacher told them to clean up. They did not leave trash at the park.

   Title: _____

2. There had been no rain for weeks. People were not able to water their lawns.

   Title: _____

3. Jeff saw a lost puppy in the park. He took it home and gave it food and water.

   Title: _____

> ❑ I can tell how two people, places, or things are connected in a story.
> ❑ I can tell the difference between stories, poems, and other things to read.

Elephants in the Wild

Read the story. Think about cause and effect. Answer each question.

It was a hot day. The elephants saw the water hole. They walked to it. They wanted to drink. The older elephants looked for crocodiles. There were none. The baby elephants played in the water. It was safe. They drank the water.

A hippo came. The baby elephants ran. The older elephants made loud noises with their trunks. The noise made the hippo run! The watering hole was safe again. The elephants liked the cool water.

1. What caused the elephants to go to the water hole?_____

   _____

2. Why did the older elephants check for crocodiles?_____

   _____

3. Why did the older elephants make noise?_____

   _____

☐   **I can ask and answer questions about what was read.**
☐   **I can retell a story.**
☐   **I can name the characters, setting, and events in a story.**

Waves

Read the story. Read each pair of sentences. Circle the sentence that tells the effect.

Most waves are not big. You can play in little waves at the beach. It can be fun!

Some waves start when there are storms at sea. The wind blows hard for a long time. The waves get bigger. They can be 80 feet (24 meters) high!

Sometimes, big storms happen. These storms are called hurricanes. They make very big waves. These waves come inland. The water can flood the streets! People have to leave the beach. The beach is not safe! People can come back to the beach later. The hurricane will end.

1. Wind blows across the water.

    Waves form.

2. The waves get bigger.

    The wind blows very hard for a long time.

3. People have to leave the beach.

    Hurricanes bring big waves into the streets.

☐ **I can ask and answer questions about what I read.**
☐ **I can tell how two people, places, or things are connected in a story.**

Name_____

What Makes You Happy?

Look at the pictures on the left. Each picture is a cause. A feeling can be an effect. Circle the face on the right that tells the effect.

Cause   **Effect**

1.

2.

3.

4.

5.

☐ I can name the characters, settings, and events in a story.
☐ I can tell how the pictures and the words go together.

Good Dog, Bad Dog

Look at each picture. What does the dog do that causes Kelly to say, "Good dog"? Write **Good dog** in the boxes under those pictures. What causes Kelly to say, "Bad dog"? Write **Bad dog** in the boxes under those pictures.

"Good dog!"

"Bad dog!"

1.

2.

3.

4.

5.

6.

❑ I can name the characters, settings, and events in a story.
❑ I can tell how the story and the pictures go together.

Name_____

Make It Rain

Read each pair of words. One word is part of a cause. The other word is part of an effect. Which is which? Write each word in the blank after **Cause** or **Effect**. Complete the sentence to tell how you know.

Example: bake, cake

Cause: __bake_____   Effect: __cake_____

How do you know? You bake the batter to get a cake!

1. rain, wet

Cause:_____   Effect: _____

How do you know? _____ makes you _____.

2. hot, sun

Cause:_____   Effect: _____

How do you know? The _____ makes you _____.

3. tree, planting a seed

Cause: _____   Effect: _____

How do you know? You must plant a _____ to grow a _____.

☐   I can ask and answer questions about what I read.
☐   I can name the characters, settings, and events in a story.

What to Wear?

You can wear a raincoat if it is a stormy day. The weather is the cause. The raincoat is the effect. Look at each cause. Circle every effect.

Cause   **Effect**

1.

2.

3.

4.

☐ I can ask and answer questions about what I read.
☐ I can name the characters, settings, and events in a story.

Name_____

What Happens?

Read each pair of sentences. Write **C** on the line by the sentence that tells about the cause. Write **E** on the line by the sentence that tells about the effect.

1. The wind blows hard. _____

    Dust is in the air. _____

2. The balloon pops. _____

    Rosa blows more and more air into the balloon. _____

3. The clown keeps falling down. _____

    Everyone laughs. _____

4. We need the perfect book. _____

    We go to the library. _____

5. I turn on the lamp. _____

    It is bright in the room. _____

☐   **I can ask and answer questions about what I read.**

Name_____

How Would You Feel?

Look at each cause. Draw a line to match each cause to the correct effect.

Cause	**Effect**

1.

A.

2.

B.

3.

C.

4.

D.

❑ I can ask and answer questions about what I read.

Rain, Rain, Go Away

Read each pair of sentences. Write **C** on the line by the sentence that tells about the cause. Write **E** by the sentence that tells about the effect.

1. There were lots of puddles. _____

    It rained for three days. _____

2. Shawn's mom drove him home from school. _____

    She had to put the car away. _____

3. Shawn had to wipe his feet. _____

    There was mud on Shawn's shoes. _____

4. The spider climbed up the wall. _____

    The rain filled up the spider's home. _____

❑ **I can ask and answer questions about what I read.**

Weather Report

A weather report causes you to decide what to wear for the day. What you wear is the effect. Read each weather report. Circle the correct effect.

Cause   **Effect**

1. Today will be sunny and warm.
   What will you wear?

_____

2. Today will be cooler. It will rain in the morning. What will you wear?

_____

3. Today will be cold. It might snow.
   What will you wear?

❑   I can ask and answer questions about what was read.
❑   I can tell how the pictures and the words go together.

The Monkey and the Tiger

Read the story. Complete each sentence by circling the correct cause.

The jungle animals had a party. It was the monkey's special day. Everyone sang and danced. The monkey did tricks. All the animals cheered! Her tricks were great! The tiger wanted everyone to cheer for him. The tiger tried to do tricks. The animals did not cheer. He did not know tricks!

1. The animals had a party because

   A. it was fun.   B. it was the monkey's special day.

2. The animals clapped and cheered for the monkey because

   A. her tricks were great.   B. it was her special day.

3. The animals did not clap for the tiger because

   A. he looked so silly.   B. he could not do the monkey's tricks.

☐ I can ask and answer questions about what was read.
☐ I can name the characters, settings, and events of the story.

What Happened?

Draw a line to match each effect to the correct cause.

Effect

Cause

1. Kate was all wet because

A. I threw his ball.

2. Joe's dad was angry because

B. she was thirsty.

3. My dog Scruff ran because

C. Joe left his bike outside.

4. Keisha asked for a glass of water because

D. his mom made pizza.

5. Toby smiled because

E. it began to rain.

Sound Effects

Sound can be a cause. Read the effects. Draw a line to match each effect to the correct cause.

Effect

1. Dusty ran to Jason

2. José lined up with the kids in his class

3. The soccer teams stopped playing

4. The cowboys picked up their plates and cups

Cause

A. when the school bell rang.

B. when the cook rang the dinner bell.

C. when Jason whistled for him.

D. when the coach blew the whistle.

❑ I can ask and answer questions about what was read.
❑ I can name the characters, settings, and events of the story.

Name_____

Cold Hands

A **cause** is what makes something happen. An **effect** is what happens. Read each pair of sentences. Write **C** in front of the sentence that tells the cause. Write **E** in front of the sentence that tells the effect.

1. _____ Tom was cold.

   _____ He rubbed his hands together.

2. _____ Tom rubbed even harder.

   _____ Rubbing made his hands warm. But, he wanted them warmer!

3. _____ He rubbed faster.

   _____ That made his hands hot!

❏   I can ask and answer questions about what was read.

Pets

Read each sentence. To find the effect, ask, "What happened?" To find the cause, ask, "Why?" Write the cause and the effect for each sentence.

1. Miguel's dog wagged his tail when Miguel poured food into a dish.

   What happened? Effect: _____

   Why? Cause: _____

2. Mary was happy when her cat climbed down the tree.

   What happened? Effect: _____

   Why? Cause: _____

3. Quan's hamster climbed a toy ladder to get cheese.

   What happened? Effect: _____

   Why? Cause: _____

☐   I can ask and answer questions about what was read.
☐   I can name the characters, settings, and events of the story.

Where Would You Go?

Look at each shopper's list. Look at the stores. Where should each person shop? Write the correct store's number on the line.

A. Zach needs:

eggs
milk
bread _____

B. Kayla needs:

kitty litter
dog food
hamster cage _____

C. Juanita needs:

cold pills
cough drops
thermometer _____

D. José needs:

gumdrops
lollipops
candy bars _____

E. Evan needs:

nails
saw
hammer _____

F. Malia needs:

pizza
soda
salad _____

☐ I can tell how the story and the pictures go together.
☐ I can compare characters and various events.

Who Needs to Sneeze?

Look at each animal. The animals have colds. Circle **Yes** or **No** for each sentence.

1. A bird with a cold goes to a nest to nap.   Yes   No

2. Both the bird and the frog could use leaves as tissues.   Yes   No

3. A bunny can climb a tree to sleep.   Yes   No

4. A frog that coughed could shake up the sea.   Yes   No

☐ I can ask and answer questions about what was read.
☐ I can compare characters and events from different stories.

What Am I Doing?

Read each story. Infer the answer to each question.

Sue Lee rode to the store. She rode up a big hill. She had to pump hard. It was easy to go down the other side. Sue Lee went very fast. She had to use her brakes!

1.   What did Sue Lee ride to the store?

a horse   a skateboard   a bike

What clues helped you infer the answer? _____

Sam likes to swing the bat. Sam can hit the ball. He loves to run to first base. Sometimes, he even makes it to third. He wants to play shortstop when he grows up!

2.   What game does Sam like?

football   baseball   golf

What clues helped you infer the answer? _____

❑   I can ask and answer questions about what was read.
❑   I can retell a story.
❑   I can name the characters, settings, and events in a story.

What Will David Do?

Read the story. Use clues in the sentences to infer the answers to the questions.

David has to move. His dad has a new job in the city. David has to pack all of his toys. He will give the old ones away. He will put the new ones in a big box. He will have to say good-bye to his friends. David will not be able to play in the barn anymore. This makes him sad.

1. Do you think David lives in the city right now? _____ Why or why not?

   _____

   _____

2. What do you think David will do with the new toys? _____

   _____

   Why?_____

   _____

3. Do you think David will miss his friends? _____ Why or why not?

   _____

   _____

☐ I can ask and answer questions about what was read.
☐ I can retell a story.
☐ I can name the characters, settings, and events in a story.

Time to Get Up!

Look at each picture. Cut out the pictures. Glue them on another piece of paper in the correct order. Then, answer the question.

1.   How did you know the correct order of the pictures? _____

_____

❑   I can retell a story.
❑   I can name the characters, settings, and events in a story.
❑   I can tell how the story and the pictures go together.

What Am I?

Katie planned a guessing game for her friends. Read each clue. Draw a line to match the clue to the correct picture.

1. I am round and orange.
   You might give me a grin.
   I make a great pie.

A.

2. Do not slip on my peel!
   I am green before I am ripe.
   I am yellow when I am good to eat.

B.

3. I am the color of snow.
   I keep my fur very clean.
   I purr when I am happy.

C.

4. I have a nose. I have a tail.
   If you ride on my back,
   we will gallop along the trail.

D.

5. I keep the sun out of your eyes.
   You might wear me as you
   round up a herd of cattle.

E.

❑ I can tell how two people, places, or things are connected in a story.
❑ I can tell how the story and the pictures go together.
❑ I can compare two stories.

In the City

What do people do in the city? Cut out the small pictures. Glue each picture where it belongs in the big picture of the city. Answer the question.

1.   How did you know where to paste the pictures? _____

_____

☐   I can name the characters, settings, and events in a story.
☐   I can tell how the story and the pictures go together.

Ready for School

Look at the pictures. Circle each school item to use inside. Draw a line to match each item to a student.

A.

B.

C.

D.

E.

F.

RED   YELLO   BLUE

G.

J.

I.

H.

☐ I can tell how the story and the pictures go together.

Which Toy Do You Want?

Draw a line to match each child to the correct toy. Answer the questions.

1.

rattle

2.

doctor's bag

3.

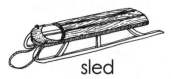
sled

4.

beach ball

5.

basketball

6. Which toy did the boy in the swimsuit want? _____

   How do you know? _____

7. Which toy does the girl dressed as a doctor want?_____

   How do you know? _____

❑ I can answer questions about key details.
❑ I can tell how the story and the pictures go together.

84

What Is Happening?

Look at the pictures in each row. Circle the picture on the right that shows what happens next.

 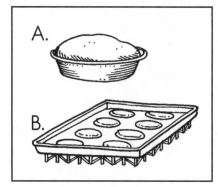

Circle the picture above that gives you clues about what the boy is making.

Circle the picture above that gives you clues about which animal the girl is feeding.

Circle the picture above that gives you clues about which plant will grow.

- ☐ I can name the characters, settings, and events in a story.
- ☐ I can tell how the story and the pictures go together.

Which Comes First?

Look at the pictures. They are not in order. Write **1** beside the picture that comes first. Write **2** beside the picture that comes next. Write **3** beside the picture that comes last.

_____

_____

_____

❑   I can tell how the story and the pictures go together.

What Comes Next?

Look at the pictures in each row. Draw a picture that shows **what happens next.**

1.

Which clues tell you what happens next? _____

_____

_____

2.

Which clues tell you what happens next? _____

_____

_____

❑ I can name the characters, settings, and events in a story.
❑ I can tell how the story and the pictures go together.

The Snowman

Read each sentence. Write **1** beside the sentence that comes first. Number the rest of the sentences in the correct order.

_____ The snowman melted away.

_____ Our lawn had a new coat of white snow.

_____ We built a snowman.

_____ The warm sun came out.

_____ Big, fat flakes of snow came down.

❏   **I can name the characters, settings, and events in a story.**

Name_____

The Missing Word

Read each sentence. Look at the picture. Use the picture to infer the correct word from the word bank. Write it on the line.

Word Bank

| bat | clown | coat | hen | nap |

1. The boy's baseball _____ is under his chair.

2. The _____ in the barn has some chicks.

3. I put on my new _____ .

4. The funny _____ had a big red nose.

5. The baby needs to take a _____ .

☐ I can ask and answer questions about what was read.
☐ I can tell how the story and the pictures go together.

Summer Fun

Look at the pictures on the bottom of the page. Cut out each picture that belongs at the beach. Glue it to the big picture.

☐ I can tell how the story and the pictures go together.

The Missing Word

Look at the picture Circle the things that do not belong in the park. Answer the questions.

Name one thing that does not belong. _____

_____

How do you know it does not belong on the playground? _____

_____

❑   **I can tell how the story and the pictures go together.**

Answer Key

Page 12
Answers will vary but may include: 2. Baby Takes a Nap; 3. Paul Runs a Race; 4. Sammy at the Park.

Page 13
1. Gingerbread Man; 2. Itsy Bitsy Spider; 3. Little Red Hen; 4. Baby Bear

Page 14
1. three bears and a girl; 2. a woman; 3. a girl and a wolf

Page 15
1. a baby fox, 2. a home for a fox; 3. the woods

Page 16
1. Circle: castle; 2. Box: cave; 3. Cross out: nest; 4. Underline: playground

Page 17
Answers will vary, but appropriate settings should be drawn around characters.

Page 18
Cross out: 1. cow; 2. dinosaur; 3. horse; 4. bathtub; 5. tree

Page 19
happy: campfire, castle, beach scene, woman with cookies; sad: cat in tree, abandoned house, ripped toy, melting snowman

Page 20
January, B; February, A; May, D; July, E; October, C; November, F

Page 21
1. ball, water; 2. bats, clouds; 3. ice, trees; 4. rocket, stars

Page 22
1. Today; 2. Future; 3. Long Ago; 4. Today

Page 23
1. forest; 2. outer space

Page 24
1. Chan; 2. Pedro; 3. Mary; 4. Keesha; 5. Ted

Page 25
Circle: 1. dog; 2. boy; 3. girl

Page 26
Circle: 1. girl; 2. boy; 3. girl; 4. girl; 5. boy

Page 27
Circle: 1. Kami; 2. Myong; 3. Ruff; Underline: 1. Kami Makes a Mask; 2. Myong Flies a Kite; 3. Ruff Finds a Bone

Page 28
Circle: 1. friends; 2. special; Color pictures that show two friends (may also include bus).

Page 29
Circle: 1. boy; 2. pencil, crayons, pencil box; 3. school

Page 30
Circle: 1. Josie Grows Up; 2. She grew older. 3. five years old; 4. school

Page 31
Circle and write: 1. home; 2. trees; 3. ground; 4. caves

Answer Key

Page 32
Circle: 1. Helpful Senses;
2. five; 3. ear; 4. nose

Page 33
1. Answers will vary but
may include: The Months
of the Year. 2. Answers
will vary but may
include: Most months
have 30 or 31 days.
3. A leap year happens
every four year when
February has 29 days.

Page 34
Answers will vary but
may include: Both get
scared. 2. They hide
under rocks or in
tunnels. 3. This article
is about spiders called
tarantulas.

Page 35
1. A man named John
Chapman who planted
apple seeds; 2. He grew
apple trees.
3. The author wrote
this to show why it was
important that Johnny
brought apple seeds to
the West.

Page 36
Circle: 1. a poster; 2. a
girl; Pictures should show
an orange, black, and
white cat named Sassy.

Page 37
X in circles: 1. What
Makes Day and Night;
2. Earth and the
Seasons; 3. Both are
about Earth and the sun.

Page 38
1. Answers will vary but
may include: "The Days
of the Week." 2. Answers
will vary but may
include: Sunday was
named after the sun.

Page 40
1. ants; 2. ladybugs;
3. grasshoppers;
4. Answers will vary
but may include:
explorecount; 5. bugs

Page 41
Any three: swings, slide,
bars, merry-go-round

Page 42
Color: 1. girl; 2. pizza;
3. pizza

Page 43
collar, bed, dog dish

Page 44
A: 2, 5, 8, 9; B: 1, 6, 7;
Circle for both: 3, 4

Page 45
Circle: 1. same;
2. different; 3. same;
4. different; 5. different;
6. same; 7. same;
8. different

Page 46
Leaves not colored: leaf
4; leaf 2; leaf 5; leaf 1;
leaf 3

Page 47
1. leaves; 2. eggs; 3. baby
birds

Page 48
Circle: A. moon; B. tent;
C. paintbrush; Answers
will vary.

Page 49
Color the flags. Circle:
1. circle; 2. leaf; 3. yellow

Page 50
1. too cold; 2. too hot;
3. too hot; 4. too cold;
5. too hot

Answer Key

Page 51
1. Sally, Rosa; 2. Chung, Matt; 3. Andre; 4. Chung, Matt; 5. Mike

Page 52
Cross out: 1. boat; 2. man; 3. tin; 4. got; 5. jam; 6. sat; 7. dog; 8. mop

Page 53
3, 5, 4, 1, 2; Circle: 1. taller; 2. shortest; 3. shorter; 4. tallest

Page 54
1. Answers will vary but may include: The author writes the story and the illustrator makes the art for the story.

Page 55
1. Answers will vary but may include: It cannot fit on city bus.
2. Answers will vary but may include: It is as long as a car.
3. Answers will vary but may include: It is shorter than a tiger shark.
4. Answers will vary but

may include: It may weigh as much as a train. 5. Answers will vary. 6. Answers will vary.

Page 56
2 Legs: hen, bird, man; 4 Legs: dog; 6 Legs: ladybug, ant

Page 57
City: 1, 5, 6; Country: 2, 3, 4

Page 58
1. bear; 2. seal; 3. giraffe; 4. Answers will vary but may include: A writer writes the riddles and an illustrator makes the art.

Page 59
1. C; 2. D; 3. E; 4. A; 5. F; 6. B

Page 60
1. Kids Clean Up; 2. Grass Turns Brown; 3. Boy Saves Dog

Page 61
1. It was a hot day; 2. to make sure it was safe; 3. to scare a hippo at the watering hole

Page 62
Circle: 1. Waves form.
2. The waves get bigger.
3. People have to leave the beach.

Page 63
Circle: 1. happy face; 2. sad face; 3. sad face; 4. sad face; 5. happy face

Page 64
1. Good Dog; 2. Good Dog; 3. Good Dog; 4. Bad Dog; 5. Bad Dog; 6. Bad Dog

Page 65
1. Cause: rain; Effect: wet; Rain makes you wet.
2. Cause: sun; Effect: hot; The sun makes you hot.
3. Cause: seed; Effect: tree; You must plant a seed to grow a tree.

Page 66
Circle: 1. mittens, boots, jacket; 2. sweater, pants, shoes; 3. shorts, sunglasses, sun cap; 4. raincoat, umbrella, rain boots

Answer Key

Page 67
1. C, E; 2. E, C; 3. C, E;
4. C, E; 5. C, E

Page 68
1. B; 2. A; 3. D; 4. C

Page 69
1. E, C; 2. C, E; 3. E, C;
4. E, C

Page 70
Circle: 1. T-shirt, shorts;
2. raincoat, umbrella;
3. scarf, mittens, hat

Page 71
Circle: 1. B; 2. A; 3. B

Page 72
1. E; 2. C; 3. A; 4. B; 5. D

Page 73
1. C; 2. A; 3. D; 4. B

Page 74
1. C, E; 2. E, C; 3. C, E

Page 75
1. Effect: His dog wagged his tail. Cause: Miguel poured food. 2. Effect: Mary was happy. Cause: Her cat climbed down from a tree. 3. Effect: The hamster climbed

a ladder. Cause: The hamster wanted some cheese.

Page 76
A. 3; B. 5; C. 6; D. 4; E. 1; F. 2

Page 77
1. Yes; 2. No; 3. No; 4. No

Page 78
1. a bike; Answers will vary but may include: She had to pump hard. 2. baseball; Answers will vary but may include: Sam uses a ball and bat to play.

Page 79
1. No, he has a barn. 2. Take them with him. He packs them up. 3. Yes, leaving makes him sad.

Page 80
In order: girl sleeping, sun rising, girl eating, girl on bus. 1. Answers will vary.

Page 81
1. B; 2. A; 3. D; 4. E; 5. C

Page 82
A. fire station; B. school;
C. post office;
D. grocery store.
1. Answers will vary.

Page 83
Circle: A, B, C, E, F, H, I, J. Match: A to girl at bulletin board; B to girl at desk with lined paper; C to boy at chalkboard; E to boy with pencil; F to girl with paintbrush; H to girl holding hands out; I to girl with computer mouse; J to boy standing with paper.

Page 84
1. sled; 2. beach ball;
3. rattle; 4. doctor's bag or first aid kit;
5. basketball; 6. beach ball, He is wearing a bathing suit; 7. doctor's bag, She is wearing a doctor's coat.

Page 85
Circle: 1. B; 2. C; 3. E; cookie cutter, bag of dog food, seed packet

Answer Key

Page 86
In order: 2, 1, 3

Page 87
1. Answers will vary.
2. Answers will vary.

Page 88
In order: 5, 2, 3, 4, 1

Page 89
1. bat; 2. hen; 3. coat;
4. clown; 5. nap

Page 90
Cut and glue: sand castle, beach ball, sailboat, fish

Page 91
Circle: giraffe, rocket ship, tractor, turkey, moon, baby, sled;
1. Answers will vary but may include: The giraffe does not belong.
2. Answers will vary but may include: It belongs in the wild.